Lights Out!

A Collection of Ghost Stories and Personal Experiences with the Paranormal

By

Vickie Lee Johnson

AuthorHouse™
1663 Liberty Drive
Bloomington, IN 47403
www.authorhouse.com
Phone: 1 (800) 839-8640

Published by AuthorHouse 09/28/2018

ISBN: 978-1-4033-2367-5 (sc)
ISBN: 978-1-4033-2366-8 (e)

Print information available on the last page.

Articles and Obituaries were taken from the Bedford Times-Mail Daily newspaper of Bedford, Indiana. Ghost stories were gathered from residents, friends, family, and coworkers in the Bedford area.

Dedication

In loving memory of my brothers

Robert Merle Johnson

12 / 25 / 73

Anthony Merle Johnson, Jr.

5 / 15 / 79 - 5 / 17 / 79

Acknowledgments

I would like to thank the following:

My mom for her encouragement and joining me on a few of my adventures.

My dad for his support and helping me put this book together.

My brother, sister, and friends for sharing their stories and feelings about the spiritual world.

Ghost Stories Contents:

Personal Experiences Contents:

Bibliography

Dixon, Henry.

Bedford Daily Mail, Death Came Suddenly To Dixon Agency Of Death Is A Mystery, 7-23-1903

Fullen, Julius.

Bedford Daily Mail, Julius Fullen Killed By Train Near Ft. Ritner and Joseph F. Kennedy Dies In Auto Accident, 8-7-1933

Kinser, Tammy.

Bedford Times Mail, Speed blamed in fatal crash, 7-12-1995

McArthur, Dennis Scott.

Bedford Times Mail, Body of young man is found in two-story house, 4-12-1976

Bedford Times Mail, Dead youth stirred controversy, 4-15-1976

Stepp Cemetery
Martinsville, In.

Some years ago, this area was the sight of the gruesome accident involving a young couple. The girl had a curfew and a strict mother. The boy who liked the girl very much was determined to get the girl home on time. In hopes to continue seeing her. Well time was lost and they were in a rush to get home. The boy was speeding down the rather curvy strip of road, lost control of his car and crashed. The girl was decapitated and the boy was killed instantly.

Several teenagers have claimed to have seen the girl's mother since she died of grief some time after the accident. She's been known to approach parked cars knocking on their windows, shaking her finger at them. She's always been seen wearing a black dress. Hanging from her neck is the battered head of her daughter.

The cemetery holds the spirit of a woman who watches over her baby's grave. Some say she sits on a chair made from stone. Others claim they have seen her sitting on a bench that's been carved from a tree trunk. This woman has watched over her child's grave in life as well as now in death. Legend has it that the chair and bench carry death omens.

A group of teenagers went to this cemetery mainly to find a good drinking spot. One girl who was lingering behind them, found herself being tapped on the shoulder. When she turned around, she was face to face with an elderly woman. The woman promised the girl that death would come to whom ever bothered the chair, then vanished. The girl ran to the others, who had already started drinking, telling them what she had just seen. They chose to ignore her warning. One of the guys thought it would be funny to dance on what he thought was the grave site, while mocking her. He died two weeks later in a car accident. Was this coincidence? His friends aren't so sure. In fact, none of them have returned to the cemetery since.

Haunted House
Bartlettsville, In.

A couple of friends of mine shared their experience with a house they believed to be haunted. Things seem to happen immediately. They would think up explanations for the occurrence, until they had none. Day after day things seem to grow more intense. Clothes and jewelry would disappear. Footsteps could be heard from the basement. Doors would slam shut. A Bible that was placed on the floor in front of the basement door, was found sitting on the coffee table in the living room.

Two weeks to the day they moved in marked the worst of the disturbances. It began around 11:30 PM and lasted until 5 AM. Footsteps started in the basement, stomping up and down the stairs. Loud banging started on the walls in the living room. A sound like machinery turning itself on and off was heard coming from the basement. Cold spots were felt throughout the house. The feeling of a presence was very strong. Both girls claimed to have seen something looking through the back bedroom window at them. As it stared at them it seemed to sink in the ground rather than just simply vanish.

The next morning they went to the landlord about their sleepless night and asked for the history of the property. The landlord told them that his father had died in the house and that they weren't the first tenants to come to him about the same disturbances. He told them that he wouldn't doubt his father is still in his workshop in the basement. After all, that's were he liked to spend most of his time. The girls moved shortly after.

Two Haunted Houses
Kurtz, In.

In a period of two weeks, my friend Louise, had to move twice, both for the same reason. The houses were haunted.

The first was a two-story fixer upper, located on a dead end road. Louise noticed things that were out of the ordinary taking place the very first night. She was having trouble falling asleep. When in the distance she could hear faint crying. Louise decided to investigate the sound. As she opened the bedroom door the sound stopped. As she approached the stairs leading to the attic, she saw what appeared to be a blood stain in the carpet. After scrubbing the spot, thinking it was gone, it reappeared. Curious, Louise lifted the carpet, before her was a pool of blood. She cleaned the hardwood surface the best she could. Night after night, for about a week, the same events would taking place. She decided it was time to go to her realtor.

The realtor told her that a young girl had committed suicide in the house. The girl was pregnant and the father of her child had left her. She had hung herself in the general location where the blood was found at the foot of the attic stairs. Numerous short-term owners have also claimed to have heard the girl sobbing in the late hours of the night.

The second house, also had a story to tell. Again, all was quite until she went to bed. Just as she started to dose off, there was a loud commotion in the attic. It sounded like something being dragged across the floor. Louise went upstairs to the attic. School books and papers were found scattered all over the floor. She neatly stacked them and left. As she reached the bottom of the steps, she heard the same sound again. The next morning she went to the realtor and demanded the history on the property.

An out of work school teacher had hung himself in the attic with a chain.

Mundell Cemetery
Heltonville, In.

Brenda, an acquaintance of mine spoke of what she hopes to be her first and last paranormal experience. She and her boyfriend had parked on the road circling the cemetery about 4 am. In the instant Brenda shut off her car, something caught her eye. As she turned her head, there was an elderly man driving through the cemetery on a tractor. Her boyfriend also witnessed the event. They watched as the tractor passed through several headstones heading towards the church. In a panic they left, thinking of a logical explanation.

Immaculate House
Heltonville, In.

When you first approach this location the house looks run-down. As you get closer and look inside you get a different story. The walls appear to be freshly painted. New carpet in all the rooms. There has even been said to be new furniture. Once you enter and get the feel of the place it begins to dissolve it's perfect view. In fact, once you enter you aren't suppose to be able to get out.

A couple, both school teachers went to this location to investigate. Once they made it upstairs they found themselves jumping out of the window. The reason as to why, has never been explained. Maybe they seen something so ghastly that they leaped in a panic.

Baseball Glove
Bedford, In.

Patricia and her husband, Keith, were watching television in their den. Beside the t.v. was their grandson's toy box. On the floor next to it on the floor was his baseball glove with the ball in it's palm. While they sat Patricia and Keith noticed the glove as it began to levitate and then flip over, dropping the ball.

Later, they told their daughter about the event. She responded by throwing the glove away. Since then they haven't had anymore bizarre activity.

Beechgrove Cemetery
Bedford, In.

This cemetery holds the final resting place of my grandmother, Evelyn Ruth (Terrell - Johnson - Harper) Close. Although, she may not be doing much resting.

My mom was on her way to work around 2:30 am one morning. Since she was running short on time, she decided to take a side road, passing Beechgrove Cemetery. Catching her eye, was a woman dressed in a yellow suit, scarf, and glasses, identical to one of my grandmother's favorite outfits. My mom has seen this woman on numerous occasions, day and night. The woman is always seen either standing or walking around my grandmother's grave. Not to mention, she's always in the same yellow suit. My mother no longer takes this route to work since her last experience with the stranger, when she looked directly at her.

7th Street Lounge
Bedford, In.

During closing hours, it's nothing out of the ordinary to have a few unexplainable encounters.

One night, as the bartender finished up the cleaning, he locked the back and side doors. Upon returning to the counter, the doors began to open and slam shut repeatedly. He left things the way they were and went home.

One bartender recalls while closing up the bar, the sound of a woman being strangled by the side door. When he went to investigate, the sound quit.

On certain nights you can hear crying. The radio has a tendency of turning itself on and off, while unplugged. But nothing has ever been seen.

Peeking Figure
Bedford, In.

When Nola moved into her house, she found on the first night, that she wasn't alone. The house has been in her family for years. Her sister who owned it before her, claims to have had a few encounters that she found hard to explain. But chose not to speak of them.

While Nola was unpacking some boxes she decided to take a quick break before finishing up. She relaxed in her recliner and gazed at the t.v. screen. Seconds later, something caught the corner of her eye. Peeking from behind the corner was a little boy. Nola described him as looking like "Casper."

The only difference was you could see his bones. She tried everything from blinking her eyes to shaking her head, to see if the image would go away. He just stood there. Nola then told him, that he needed to go, she was busy and that he didn't belong there. With that he simply vanished.

Big Tunnel
Tunnelton, In.

Louise, who shared her story with me about the two houses in Kurtz, told me another story that is based on the death of her father. The tunnel is already popular for being haunted after the murder of Henry Dixon back in 1908. Legend has is it, that late at night you can see the image of Dixon carrying a lantern in one hand and his head under the other. He had suffered a severe blow to the head, robbed, and was then laid on the tracks to be erased. He was discovered the morning of July 23rd at 4:30 am by the day watchman.

On August 7, 1933, Julius Fullen died of a fractured skull, broken left arm, loss of several fingers on his right hand, and a severely bruised body.

According to his daughter Louise, Julius was walking the tracks en route to his home in Leesville, where he was struck by a train. He was able to crawl to a house over a mile away. The resident at first ignored him, thinking he was drunk. Then she walked into her kitchen to sneak a peak from her window and realized that he was injured. Before helped arrived he slipped into unconsciousness, he was sent to the hospital where he died undergoing emergency surgery.

Julius is also suppose to haunt the tunnel, carrying a lantern with a glowing green light. Louise once told me that if I ask, Julius just might play his fiddle for me.

Devil's Backbone
Tunnelton, In.

The legend that surrounds this strip of road will take you back to the horse and buggy days. A man and his family were killed when their horse was spooked and pulled them over the steep side of the curvy, narrow path. On occasion you can hear the screams of the man and his family as they fall to their deaths.

I've been told, that a few years back, on prom night some cheerleaders and football players went out for a cruise after the dance. They were traveling at a high speed when they missed a curve. All the bodies were recovered except one of the cheerleaders. Rumor has it, that she was pinned under some wreckage a short distance away from the others. Around midnight, you just may hear the forgotten cheerleader screaming for help.

Haunted House
Bono, In.

Mary and her husband were looking to buy a house. They made their pick in Bono. It was a fixer-upper, but it was within their budget. They made an appointment to meet with the realtor. Mary and her husband went early to overlook the outside of the place. They noticed some strange noises coming from inside the house. It sounded like furniture being moved and loud footsteps. Thinking that the realtor was inside they went to investigate. As they approached the front door the realtor pulled up in the driveway. Walking through the house there was no source found for all the commotion they had heard moments prior. Although there was a strong gas smell. Also a strong sensation of being watched. Mary and her husband both felt ill and left the house with headaches. Oddly enough, the realtor never smelt anything.

Bond's Chapel
Mitchell, In.

The first time went to Bond's Chapel I was accompanied by my friend, Alley, her husband, Mike, and my brother Dalis. We arrived around 4 pm the place was packed with people. The gravel driveway wasn't much, so the cars had to park in a zig zag formation. The chapel doors stood wide open as children played in the cemetery.

21

We hesitated about doing anything with the crowd being there. So we drove down the road to turn around and leave. As we approached the church, no one was there. It had just been seconds we were in front of the place.

There wasn't any dust from where the last car had pulled away. The way the cars had been positioned there's no way they could have left in a matter of seconds.

Alley and her husband had an experience of their own soon after. It was a rainy afternoon, as the chapel came into view, so did a strange man. The one thing that stood out about this stranger was his fluorescent vest.

He stood on the side of the road and motioned for them to come in his direction. In a panic they turned around in front of the church, then stopped to look for the man. Suddenly, he appeared on Alley side of the car beating on the window. Mike floored it, as they both looked back, no man was in sight.

The Virgin Mary statue is suppose to be a death omen. Located in the cemetery or the church itself. I have never seen it. But that doesn't mean she isn't there. If you look into her eyes you are to die within a 24 hour period.

A young couple went to check out the story. The boy asked the Virgin Mary to do her worst, using a few foul words in the mix of things. They left shortly afterwards, not expecting anything to happen. On their way home they encountered something horrifying.

When the girl came to her senses, she found herself 150 ft. from the back of the car. When questioned by the police, she really had no explanation as to what had happened.

Her boyfriend's body was found up in one of the tree tops. His head sat neatly in the driver's seat. The girl recalls traveling at a high speed, abruptly stopping, then everything went black. There was no damage to the car. It was the only thing that hadn't been touched.

Orphanage
Orleans, In.

The story goes that back in the 1800's this building was once an orphanage. One night, out of the blue, the caretakers slaughtered all the children. There is a small cemetery across the street from the building. Many claim that this is the resting place for them. When the orphanage closed its doors, it was reopened as a poor house. It has since been abandoned.

Tunnels have been said to be under the building. People who have walked through what remains have spoken of an old man. He lives in one of the upstairs rooms. As you try to open this particular door, the man appears banging on the back of it with his cane.

When the spooked come running out, the old man can usually be seen hiding behind one of the trees, watching.

Also, several dogs have been said to watch over the property. They will lead you to the front steps, where you'll hear the screams of children.

Methodist Church & Cemetery

Shoals, In.

Every Halloween the statue of a little girl is said to walk. When she returns to her grave she changes position kneeling on her opposite knee. It is creepy how she stands out, with vandals help. The touch of fire red nail polish covering her eyes.

Another note worthy story is that of an accident. A woman traveling at a high speed on the long straight stretch of road, was killed instantly, after her car suddenly stopped for no reason. A jogger found the woman, looking back towards the cemetery in the direct path of the statue.

Haunted House
Paoli, In.

This property is made of a family cemetery and an old house. Occasionally visited by a tall man dressed in a black suit.

The house has it own collection of haunts. My friend Mary told me of this place and her encounters. The kitchen floor would frequently vibrate. Sounds of a woman crying could be heard through out the house. Strange noises could be heard in the attic, yet no one was or ever had been up there.

One night the commotion was so disturbing the Mary stormed upstairs to enter the attic. One by one she began to remove nails that had held the door shut. As removed a few the door abruptly flew open. One of the nails caught on her arm, leaving a nasty cut. Following with a rush of cold air that knocked her off her feet. She picked herself up off the floor, shut the attic door, and moved out soon after.

Haunted House
Mayport, Fl.

Growing up, my family traveled quite a bit. My dad was in the military for 20 years. Although, in all that time nothing out of the ordinary ever took place. That is until we moved to Mayport Naval Base in Florida. It wasn't until my father was given his papers to transfer to New Jersey, that the disturbances began.

One afternoon, my mother and I were watching "As the World Turns." At the same time we took notice to a sound coming from the window behind us. It sounded like someone was throwing rocks at the glass. When I went outside to check the source, no one was there. As I looked through the window at my mother the window began to shake violently. It eventually quit, but the source was never found.

That event was just the beginning. The television would turn itself on and off. Doors and windows would open and close on their own. Blinds would occasionally draw themselves up and down. Our neighbors Norman and

Caroline were having problems also. Norman had come home from work one evening, out of habit, threw his keys down on his night stand. The next morning, after literally tearing the bedroom apart looking for them, found his keys on the dining room table.

I remember one time, my mom was out in the front yard talking to the neighbor. I was sitting in the living room watching cartoons. It seemed that my surroundings took on a fuzzy look. Somewhat like a dream. I could hear something moving behind me. When I turned around to face the sound, I focused on the window. There was a single blind moving. I walked up to it. It looked as if someone had a hold of it, pulling up and then pushing it back into place.

Caroline, our neighbor, liked to go to psychics and palm readers. One day she decided to bring up the little problem the she and Norman had. The psychic told her that there was a spirit in her home. It was an elderly lady dressed in a gray ruffled dress traced in lace. She's just waiting for someone to help her cross over.

My mom decided to call a friend of hers from the church. Her husband was the preacher. When they both entered the house they immediately sensed that something was wrong. Everyone gathered in the living room. They both began to pray. The doors and windows began to open and slam shut. The blinds were waving violently. The television was turning itself on and off repeatedly. When the prayer was finished so was the disturbance. The preacher's wife looked over to my mother and said that it was either the Lord coming in or the Devil moving out. That seemed to end our ordeal, at least at this house.

Haunted House
Fort Monmouth, NJ

This was the last place my dad was stationed in the military. We lived here for about 3 years. Long enough for me to get majority of my senior year done. We had unexplainable incidents hit us once we were settled in.

It all started the night my mom was making tacos. As she walked towards the microwave to thaw the hamburger, its door opened. My brother, sister, and I witnessed it. What really got our attention was when my mom shut the door and the microwave turned itself on.

The front door had a habit of coming open all by itself. Whether it was locked or not. The television done it usual turning itself on and off, which we were use to from the house before. The vcr would show it was recording when there was no tape inside. The lights would frequently flicker or grow bright then dim.

One night that is very memorable for me was when I was downstairs by myself. Everyone else was upstairs asleep. I was downstairs watching a Lizzie Borden special.

31

The only thing lighting the room was the t.v. screen. My room was the sun room. It had French doors that opened out into the living room. The couch was infront of these doors blocking them. So if I wanted to go in or out I would have to move the couch.

As I was getting involved with the show the French doors came open as far as they could, which wasn't much, and started banging up against the back of the couch. I jumped up and took a chance of sliding my hand through the doors and flipping on the light switch. All the windows were shut and locked. So I turned the light off and returned to the living room, in hopes of finishing my show. Again, the doors began to bang against the back of the couch. I decided to call it a night and went upstairs to sleep.

My brother and sister wasn't old enough at the time to understand what was going on, but they knew that it wasn't normal. My sister told some friends at school some of the strange things that had been taking place. My mom figured that one of them would use the story to there advantage. We soon left to visit my grandparents in Heltonville, In.

When we returned, my sister's school chum had a story waiting for her. A boy who lived just a few houses down the street claimed he saw something while we were out of town. He told my sister that a few nights prior he walked passed our house and saw figures standing in the windows.

He could hear screaming from inside, not to mention the curtains were waving violently. My sister was so shook up about it, she wouldn't go into the house.

She stood out in the front yard crying. So my parents went to the boys house and confronted him. He admitted on making the whole thing up. As a result he was grounded for a week.

The last thing that I can remember happening before we moved to Bedford, In. was waking up in the middle of the night with this intense feeling that someone was in the room. When I glanced up above me there was this floating black mass. I kept blinking my eyes thinking I was still asleep. As I watched, it gradually moved up towards the ceiling and vanished.

Haunted House
Bartlettsville, In.

I found this house just by cruising the back roads. I went one rainy afternoon and explored the bottom floor. I was facing the wall, dividing me from the living room. All of the sudden their was this knocking on the walls. I walked into the living room and back again, couldn't find the source, so I went outside to investigate.

I was standing in the driver's side doorway reloading my camera, I had my back facing the woods that surrounded the house. I heard footsteps coming up behind me. As turned and looked down at the ground I could see the grass being pressed down, twigs were snapping, and footprints being made.

I quickly took some pictures and got into the car. An acquaintance that was waiting for me in the car, and WAS a skeptic, looked up into the living room window and literally screamed. He was so shook up that he reached over and started the car. Then tried to stretch his leg over the gear shift to reach the accelerator. Once we were out of the driveway, I asked what the problem was. He told me when he looked through the living room window a figure floated by, made eye contact, then vanished.

The second incident involved my brother, Dalis, and I parked the car at an angle from the back door. My brother stayed in the car while I attempted to go inside. I left the car running not expecting to be there long. As I approached the back door, it appeared as if someone was pushing down on the accelerator. What worried me was that I was standing in front of the car. The closer I got to the back door, the louder the acceleration would be. Then Dalis yelled out for me to get back in the car. He pointed out my keys swaying rapidly on the key ring. I covered them with my hand, to stop them from swinging. Once, I opened my hand they began to swing violently, like someone or something was hitting them hard. As we started to leave the car began to shake, this lasted until we reached the blacktop in front of the house. It has since been torn down.

Haunted House
Heltonville, In.

This house and the property it sits on has a very negative past. It all began April 12, 1976, when the body of 18 year old Dennis Scott Mc Arthur was found. His half naked body draped with a blanket was found lying on the couch. He was discovered by his mother, sister, and brother-in-law.

In an article printed in the Bedford Times Mail, April 15, 1976, it was declared that the cause of death was exposure and malnutrition. His mother was returning home from a 4 month voluntary commitment in the Madison State Hospital. She found him lying in a fetal position along with spattered blood on the floor and walls.

Dennis Scott Mc Arthur had made a name for himself as a juvenile delinquent.

1. Driving a vehicle without a license.
2. Illegal possession of alcohol.
3. Fleeing a police officer.
4. Curfew violation.
5. Carrying a concealed weapon.

On April 18, 1976, an article was written on the condition of Mc Arthur's surroundings as they were discovered the morning of the 12th. Plus, information from the coroner.

1. Furniture had been tipped over.
2. House was filthy.
3. Cold, dry blood was on walls and floor.
4. ½ Can of moldy beans was in the fridge.
5. Change scattered on the floor.

Dennis hadn't eaten for days, possibly weeks prior to his death. No trace of food or drugs was found in his digestive system.

April 29, 1976, an article identifies the type of blood discovered.

The blood found at the scene was human Type O. Large spots of it were found beside, behind, and on the front of the couch. They were on opposite ends from where the body was found. Also found on the front door and on 3 small pieces of wood.

May 16, 1976, Three pills were found and have been identified. Also, a theory to Mc Arthur's death.

1. Cogentin, used to treat Parkinson's disease.
2. Prolixin, depressant.
3. Unnamed megavitamin energy pill.

Theory:

Dennis took some kind of drug mixed with alcohol, throwing him into a coma, lasting until his death of malnutrition.

May 27, 1978, another body was discovered on the property. Gerry Lee, 28, was found hanging from a rather low branch from a tree that stands in the front yard of this location. His feet were touching the ground and his knees were buckled. Bizarre circumstances surround his death as well.

Since these events have happened, the house was left abandoned, occasionally used for practicing of witchcraft or devil worship. Within the last couple of years the property has found new ownership and the house burnt down. My Uncle John claimed to had been one of many attending as they burnt the place down. He as well as others witnessed images taking form in the smoke as the house disintegrated.

My brother, Dalis, my friend, Alley and her husband Mike accompanied me a few times. The first time we went to this location, things began to happen almost immediately. As we looked around to get the feel of the atmosphere we noticed dried blood on the walls, a dresser, and on a curtain hanging from the kitchen door. The floor was falling through the walls were covered with spray paint. One of the walls had threats to certain individuals. The attic was cluttered with old newspapers and junk. There also was a noose hanging from one of the ceiling beams.

Alley entered the kitchen, almost immediately started yelling for me. She had noticed a decrease in the temperature and could feel something cold circling her. As I walked into the doorway, I was pushed back into the dining room. Mike and Dalis seemed to stand in shock. I felt like I had been hit with a sheet of ice. I hesitated on attempting it again. Meanwhile, Alley is standing in the middle of the room, noticing that the cold swirl of energy was moving towards the stairway leading to the attic. It slowly moved up the stairs, where we followed and found nothing out of the ordinary.

One night Dalis, Jim, and I went to the house. Usually I would park on the dirt path in front. This time we decided to park the car next to the house in the overgrown weeds. Jim's car had several problems, one being the gear shift sticking. Of coarse in the thrill of it all, this very thing happens.

Here it is 12:30 am, and we are stuck in the middle of Heltonville. Dalis and I sat in the car while Jim got out trying to fix it. Dalis looked up at the second story window where he noticed a large dark figure with a glowing light behind it.

It appeared to grow in size, bigger than the window itself. We couldn't make out any detail in image. It seemed to put its hands on its hips and continue to grow. Either that or it was getting closer.

Thankfully, the car decided to move. Just as we approach the main back road the car dies. Jim gets out again, to fix it. When he returned, he was white as a sheet. He said that he could hear voices. They seemed to be coming from the corn fields surrounding us. I didn't bother to get out and investigate looking at him was enough for me.

There was one trip with Dalis that I found to be nerve wrecking. I had pulled up on the dirt driveway, not thinking I turned off my car. My starter was slowly going out of my car. So if we were to get in a jam it was safe to say that we weren't going anywhere.

We sat in the car for a while making conversation, hoping something would happen. Suddenly, we could hear moaning coming from inside the crumbling house. Dalis was still in the car when I made my discovery. Two big dogs at the start of the dirt path. I quickly got back into the car.

Once, I calmed down we both attempted to get out. Looking at the rear view mirror the two dogs were still behind us. Once we got out, they had vanished.

One afternoon, I went to Heltonville to get some pictures of the rope used to hang a young boy in 1978. I had reached out to touch the bottom of the rope as it began to dissolve in my hand. Dalis was about 75 ft away from me, when a voice caught my attention.

As, I walked back towards the car and motioned to Dalis that we were leaving, I heard the voice again. This time it sounded more stern. It was plainly telling me to "GO!." This demand continued until, I was in my car. Dalis seemed puzzled, as to why, I was in such a rush to leave.

He was later thankful that I hadn't said anything to him until we left.

Crossroads Church
Needmore, In.

Behind the church is a patch of woods that have been rumored to be used for devil worship. I've heard that tools used for sacrifice can be found in the depth of it all. Jim and I went out there one evening to look around. It seemed to be the perfect mood for things.

Clear night, full moon, and some bad vibes. I was sitting on the hood of the car, while Jim was inside cursing his new CD player for not working. After a few minutes, he decided to give up. As he went to shut his door, the car began to roll backwards. With me still on the hood.

What got my attention more than anything, was at the very moment my feet touch the ground, the car stopped rolling. In attempt to leave, the car didn't want to start. Once it did, it didn't want to move. The tires just seem to spin. I had volunteered to get out to see if maybe we were hung up. About that time, the back of the car seemed to lift off the ground. He continued to give the car gas. As the panic began to show between the two of us, the car seemed to drop and we flew out of there.

On the highway, we appeared to be flying by cars and gaining speed. I told him he could slow down. He then turned on his dome light and showed me that his feet where no where near the pedals. It was more like we were being pushed.

Quarry

Needmore, In.

A few years ago a group of men dragged a young woman into the depth of the quarry. There they raped, beat, and decapitated her. It is rumored that if you go to the quarry around midnight she will appear. Although there are some guidelines to this on.

1. If there is a man in the car, she'll try to attack him.
2. If there's just a woman in the car, she'll appear, but do no harm.
3. If she doesn't appear whether or not a man is in the car, she'll make her presence know. Usually by tampering with your car.

One man described his experience quite frightening. He had drove to the location alone. He turned off his car and proceeded to walk through the quarry. He then heard a scream that he found to be spine tingling. He then started back to his car.

Once he reached it, both sides had been scratched up. He said it looked like fingernails were the source. He got into his car and attempted to start it. Again and again the car wouldn't start. As the screams grew louder and closer he looked over to their direction. There he saw the figure of a woman, he described her as an outline, her head under one arm, the head still shrieking.

The image slowly moved towards the vehicle. As she reached out for the front of it, his car started and he quickly left. The quarry starts in Oolitic and stretches for about 7 miles into Needmore. One night I was accompanied by Jim, Tea and her boyfriend, Nick.

We'd walked the entire distance earlier that day just to see if we could sense anything. Here we sat in the car from 11 pm to 11:45 pm waiting. We decided to get out and stretch our legs. Once we got out of the car we noticed something approaching us.

It appeared to be a headless form with a bright glow behind it. We all piled up in the car and attempted to leave. It wouldn't start. While the guys focused on the car, Tea and I stared at the transparent image and listened to the thumping sound coming from the back of the car. It sounded like someone tapping on the trunk, yet no one was there. With all the excitement the car decided to start, the image instantly vanished, and the thumping had stopped.

Haunted House
Avoca, In.

After my dad retired from the Navy he decided it would be best to move closer to family. So as of May '94 we moved here.

Every member of the family has experienced something. Being my mom, dad, brother, Dalis and my sister, Evelyn.

My sister was the first to have an experience. Evelyn said it all started for her one night when she had went to the kitchen to get something to drink. Everyone else was in bed asleep. As she poured her drink she noticed that she wasn't alone.

There before her stood a man, a man who'll come to her on 2 more occasions. No one she recognized. He looked as though he wanted to communicate. His mouth was moving but nothing was coming out. Once he had finished lipping what he was trying to say he vanished.

The second time Evelyn saw him was in the afternoon. She went outside to get something out the garage. One her way back into the house, she glanced over towards my dad's truck. Standing there was the same man. Evelyn decided not to stick around and went back inside the house.

The third and last time she saw him, she was watching t.v. in the living room. She was lying down and went to reposition herself. Once she did she saw the man standing beside the t.v. looking down at her.

Evelyn chose to ignore the figure and continued watching t.v. After a few moments she looked over to where he was standing, he had gone...

September 13, 1997, marked the start of some strange events. My grandma, Evelyn Close, had died in her apartment, she was found 24 hours later. When my parents and I arrived they had just removed her body.

There were about 20 + family members trying to cram themselves in her one bedroom apartment. When my mom and I crossed the threshold we felt this energy pushing between the two of us. It was like someone wanted to get out of there. It was then I told my mom I had to leave. It was just too crowded.

My sister, Evelyn, has been the only one to actually see my grandma since her passing. My mom claims it has to do with Evelyn being her name sake. Most of the activity we believe to be my grandma has taken place in the basement. Probably because we have majority of her belongings down there.

Her antique desk, diaries, and other personal items. When my sister first seen her she appeared to her as a grainy outline, like sand. When communication was attempted my grandma began to dissolve. The last thing she saw of her was a curl of her hair.

My dad and Uncle was downstairs working in the wood shop. They had decided to call it a night around 2:30 am. They went upstairs to get a snack. My dad had returned downstairs for something he had forgot. He found a small brown paper bag, that belonged to my grandma sitting on the table. When he lifted the bag the saw dust hadn't been disturbed. It had been sitting on top of his shelf, along with a few other things of hers. My dad yelled for my mom and Uncle to come downstairs. He opened the bag to find 3 pictures fanned out on the bottom of the bag. One was a shot of my dad in his military uniform. Another was of my Uncle Derek, and the third was of my mom and us kids. They decided to go upstairs, quickly.

Late one night, my sister was sitting on the floor at the end of her bed. She sat patiently watching T.V. and she waited for a phone call from her boyfriend, Sid. Her remote, that had been sitting in the middle of the bed, flew off, hit the screen, and then landed beside her.

My brother, was sitting in the living room talking to a friend on the phone. Something caught his eye in the family room by the french doors. He looked over, and explained what he had seen, as a vortex. He then added that it began to grow in size. He then hung up on his friend, and quickly ran to his room.

My sister for a while seemed to be the center of attention. She would see a white mass on a regular basis. It lacked detail and would usually dart into a corner when she would enter the room. It usually appears between 8 pm - 9 pm. Sid came over one night and seen something he couldn't explain. He waited until he got home before telling my sister. While they spoke on the phone, Evelyn was sitting on the floor. She was facing her bedroom door and her back resting against the side of the bed. Sid went on with his story which was the same as Evelyn's.

Out of the corner of her eye, she saw what she described as a white blob. It then darted over into the far corner. In the midstream of doing this, it brushed up against her face. As she looked over in its direction, she could make out very faint detail. Out of everything that has happened to her, this was the only encounter that scared her.

Sid had one encounter that was kind of hard to ignore. He had spilled his drink in the kitchen. After cleaning up the mess, he attempted to open the basement door to throw the dirty towel down towards the washer. The basement door wouldn't open. So he yelled for my mom, sister, and brother.

None of them could get the door to budge. Finally, it came open banging against the wall behind it. Dalis pointed down the steps. There was this blue ball just hovering. He then pushed Sid out of the way and proceeded downstairs after it. He chased it through three rooms. Losing it as it passed through the door leading to my dad's workshop.

A few days after my grandma passed away, my mom claims she had a visit from her. My dad had left for work it was about 5 am. She walked with him out to his truck and seen him off. She then returned to bed. She laid there, in and out of sleep.

Then she felt someone climbing in bed beside of her. Figuring my dad had changed his mind about returning to work so soon, after losing his mother. She rolled over to console him. When she did there was no one there. She then jumped out of bed and turned on the lights. There before her on my dad's side of the bed was an indention of a body.

After, I moved out for the fourth time I decided to just leave my more valued possessions in my mom's basement. One of those items being my stereo system. Sid occasionally would go downstairs to play a CD to find, that he wasn't alone.

He claimed that sometimes he would get down the stairs, not even be near the stereo and it would turn itself on. Or he could be finished listening to a CD and go to leave, when the system would shut itself off. Sometimes just to turn on again as he ran upstairs.

My dad had an experience, that made him think twice about his disbelief in the paranormal. He was down in the basement working on my computer. He worked as my mom watched trying to figure out as to why the speakers weren't working.

Sitting on the desk in front of him was some papers being braced in front of the speakers by his spittoon. As he was fixing to give up, he noticed the spittoon as it danced side to side. My dad shook his head, looked at my mom and asked if she saw it. She did.

Moments later, the spittoon slid forward, causing the papers to slide. The speakers power button could be seen, that it was turned off.

Dalis had a frightening encounter as he stepped out of the shower. He had bent over to dry his legs, as he rose up to stand straight, he found himself face to face with what he described as an angel. It stood in the corner occupying the entire space. It's wings, trimmed in gold. The sound of rustling feathers, as the figure tried to spread it's wings.

A concerned expression on it's face. Dalis quickly ran out of the bathroom into the hallway as the figure attempted to reach out to him. He then looked back, standing there was the angel, gesturing for Dalis to come back.

He waited a moment, trying to think of a logical explanation. He couldn't. He returned to the bathroom. Nothing. But the angel wasn't the only encounter Dalis was going to have that night. He describes his second figure as a man, washed in bright green light.

Dalis claims the man never tries to communicate. Just appears, on a nightly basis, sitting on Dalis' workout bench. Where he stays until Dalis falls asleep.

One night Dalis and Sid were down in the basement listening to CD's. I had a mirror wedged behind a dresser that caught Dalis' eye. He pulled it out and noticed something odd in the reflection behind him. It appeared that someone was standing on the basement stairs. But, from where they were standing, you could only see there knees down to there feet.

He called Sid's attention to it. He too only saw legs. When they turned around to see who was on the stairs, no one was there. Again, looking back in the mirror you could still see legs. On other occasions the guys have seen faces looking back at them. On any account they felt they were not alone.

Patton Hill Road
Avoca, In.

On July 11, 1995 Tammy Kinser was killed while traveling at a high speed on Patton Hill Road. Her 1991 Mercury Capri was going so fast that it was airborne before hitting a pole in Bill and Jo Strunk's front yard. Unfortunately, I got to witness this incident. It happened around 12:23 pm, that's when the 911 call was made.

I was running late for a meeting at work when I seen Tammy fly by, almost literally. She looked more like a red streak. I broke over the hill where Tammy had wrecked and didn't realize the situation. My mom had left right after me, and knew what road I had taken.

By the time she had reached the scene, police were everywhere. I remember her telling me that she asked the officer if a blue car was involved. All they told her was that they were more concerned about the person in the red one. Not really telling her that Tammy's car was the only one involved. Tammy 24, died instantly of extensive damage done to the right side of her head. She was laid to rest in Green Hill Cemetery.

Many wrecks have occurred on the road. Some bizarre sightings as well. One was witnessed by my mom. My mom was on her way to work about 2:20 am. As she approached the hill, where Tammy died, she noticed two glowing balls. They appeared to be headlights. So she slowed down and moved to the side of the narrow path. When they got right up on her they split and floated off in different directions.

The second event I seen myself. I had left my mom's house around 11:45 pm. I had reached the same spot where my mom had her experience. I saw a white female figure walk out in the middle of the road. I started up the hill, where it was standing. When my headlights hit it, The figure threw up its arms covering its face and vanished. I haven't seen it since.

Avoca Fish Hatchery
Avoca, In.

Dalis and I decided one evening to investigate the old cemetery that was in the woods behind my trailer. It was February 22, 6:50 pm. It was beginning to get dark outside. We began to walk towards the cemetery, but never actually made it.

As we got the site in view, Dalis heard a voice coming from the woods surrounding us. He then pointed his finger out, claiming he had seen a white figure peeking out from behind one of the trees. I looked, but didn't see anything.

I began to take some pictures as I proceeded to the cemetery. Dalis became frantic, when he seen the figure again, this time she was closer than before. We were both taking into consideration where she may pop up next, we chose to leave.

The cemetery rests on the top of a hill in the Avoca Fish Hatchery. It's the burial plots of the Turner family. Some of them being soldiers. They say on certain nights around midnight, you can see the deceased of this site in uniform with there wounds vividly noticeable.

Haunted Nursing Home
Bedford, In.

I have worked in this nursing home, which will remain anonymous, for about 8 years. Residents as well as staff have been touched by something they can not explain.

Room # 83 was the home of a woman, we'll call Ruth. She was a very unpleasant person. She had suddenly fell ill and after suffering for two weeks, died on her 87th birthday.

According to night shift, they started seeing an apparition, fitting Ruth's description. Bed check's had been done and the CNA's gathered at the nurses station to speak with the nurse.

One of the girls, we'll call Jennifer, glanced down the hallway, seeing a woman in a wheelchair staring back at her. The woman had pushed herself from what was Ruth's room, across the hall, and back again.

Before entering the room she glanced back up at the girls sitting in disbelief at the nurses station. Here it was pushing 11 pm, everyone was asleep.

When a woman, we'll call Lorie, moved into Ruth's old room, she got more than she bargained for. Lorie, was aware of her surroundings and was coherent enough to let us know if she needed anything.

One night, Lorie broke the silence of the night by a shrilling scream. She was pointing up towards the left corner of the ceiling. She began to holler, "There, There!!!" She then began to follow the movement of what she was seeing, with here finger. According to her, it left the corner of the ceiling, traveled through the room, and into the wall in the hallway.

Room # 80 at one time was the home of my great grandma, Beulah Johnson. But since then it has had many occupants. I had just finished answering the call light in this room when I was stopped by 2 coworkers. I was standing in the doorway facing the hallway. The privacy curtain was pulled up against the wall beside me. As we talked, the curtain wrapped itself around my arm with a tight grip. My coworkers just stood there, looked over at each other, then literally made a mad dash down the hallway. I snatched back the curtain, to find no one there.

West Hall Room # 1 is known to the majority of the staff, as the most haunted room in the building. A coworker, we'll name Sharon, was the only CNA on the floor. Her help had went to break when the resident in room # 1 passed away.

The nurses asked Sharon to get her ready for the mortuary while they called the family. Sharon prepared herself to go into the room. She entered and walked over to the side of the bed. Before she had time to do anything, she found herself being pushed onto the floor.

There wasn't anyone else in the room. That night was Sharon's last. The room was used for storage after the incident. Now with the census increase the room is being used again.

Another story that originated from West Hall, was that of a woman whose husband had just passed away. She was lying in bed with her call light on. She was on bed rest, unable to help herself. When the CNA entered the room, she found the woman in a trance-like state. As she left, the door slammed behind her.

The CNA was able to crack the door open enough to see the woman, still in a daze, lying in bed. All of the sudden the CNA saw a man's hand reach out from behind the door, slamming it shut.

My mom used to work in the kitchen of the facility. She would go to work at 2:30 am until 11 am. One morning she entered and began to turn on the lights as she walked through. Halfway through the darkness, the radio came on.

It was on the opposite of the room. She turned on the rest of the lights, thinking someone was in there with her. By the time she got over to the radio it was blaring. She attempted to turn it down even shut it off. She decided to just work around the noise.

It then shut itself off. It made her think of a coworker that had recently died of heart complications. This coworker would always argue with the crew about what station they were going to listen to.

Unit 2 is famous for its flushing toilets, cold spots, swaying privacy curtains and black shadows. But every once and a while something out of the expected happens. A coworker was preparing to give a shower.

She stripped the residents bed. Then brought in some linens to make it up after the shower. On the mattress was a waffle air mattress. Upon returning to the room the air mattress had turned itself sideways, draping over the sides of the bed.

A few years ago in room # 352 a woman, we'll call Helen, is remembered as being very stern and having a stare that would go through you.

The night of her death marked some odd events. A Q.M.A., we'll call Nola, was taking a quick break. As she sat under the balcony of the dining room, the window of Helen's room caught her eye. Flowing out of it was a white mass. It drifted off towards the sky where it vanished. Nola quickly went inside to check on her. It was then she was given the news that Helen had just passed away.

Patricia, a CNA, went into Helen's room to prepare her for the mortuary. Patricia wasn't one of Helen's favorites. So when she entered the room, she felt quite uncomfortable.

As she started to clean Helen, she noticed that her eyes were open and seem to be fixed on Patricia. She attempted to close them several times. But time and time again they would open staring right at her.

Among the living her stare was a sign that she didn't like you. A CNA we'll call Mary, had just returned from break. She went into the utility room to fill out her assignment sheet. Sitting in front of her on the counter was a few pop cans.

There was one that caught her eye. As she watched this particular can, it began to rotate and then glided across the counter top towards her. At first she thought it was maybe sweat from the can causing it to move.

Upon inspecting, she found the can to be empty and bone dry inside as well as out.

The Linen Closet has also been a hot spot for activity. A coworker had approached the closet, just to come running to the nurses station in hysterics. She had tried to open the door, feeling the sensation that someone was pushing it against her. She stepped back, it then slammed shut. I agreed to go into the closet and get the linens she needed. The door opened with ease along with a cold brush of air coming out.

Room # 343 - After supper I began taking residents back to there rooms. Among them was a woman, we'll call Margie. I was arranging things to lay Margie down for the evening. Her roommate was still in the dining room. I pushed her roommate's privacy curtains towards the doorway and Margie's around her. I was just finishing up when I heard her roommate's curtain being drawn.

Thinking she had returned from the dining room, I greeted her. When I didn't get a response, I stepped out from behind the curtain to see that nothing had been disturbed and no one was there. As I pulled back Margie's curtains I noticed the curtains that had once been against the doorway were gliding towards me. It traveled from the door to the middle of the room. I calmly asked if it was finished. The bottom of the curtain then began to jerk in all directions. It stopped after a few seconds. I then pushed it back up against the wall and left.

I once asked Regina, a resident, if she believed in ghosts and if she had any stories she would like to share. Regina simply said that she wasn't going to say that she didn't believe in them. About two weeks later she had a story to tell. I had just clocked in and was getting things ready for bed check's. Regina stood in her doorway motioning for me to go in her room. She then began to tell me about her morning.

She had just received her medicine, when she could hear footsteps enter the room. Thinking it was the newspaper girl, she rose up to thank her. Standing at the foot of her bed was her sister-in-law. The eerie thing was that she had died the summer. Prior Regina described her as looking so happy, with a big smile.

She stood there for a few seconds then vanished. Regina is now a believer. She just needed a little convincing.

Breckinridge Cemetery
Bedford, In.

One evening after a few hours of cruising the country side, I decided to stop at this location. Accompanied by a friend who wasn't keen on the idea of walking through a cemetery.

So as we sat, he struck up a conversation on U.F.O.'s. As we argued their existence, I glanced up in my rear view mirror. There looking back at me was my great-grandmother.

She had passed away a month earlier and was buried in this cemetery. She was wearing a glowing white cloak. She bent down enough to where I eyes met in the mirror. She then cracked a smile.

I didn't even think. I remember yelling, "My grandmother is behind the car." I opened the car door and jumped out, as our eyes met she vanished.

Haunted House

Bedford, In.

September 29, 1999

This house on G Street belongs to my boyfriend's family. The house is a three bedroom and from what I've been told a relative has died in two of them and a neighbor in the other. It made me a little uncomfortable since I'm not family.

I was also very paranoid when we moved in, trying not to move anything that shouldn't be moved. I'll admit, it seemed no matter how careful I thought I was being, strange things were taking place.

It all started day one. It was about 11 pm. I had just started cleaning and was alone in the house. In the middle of dusting I heard footsteps behind me followed by a loud sigh. It sounded like someone was frustrated.

I went into the kitchen and turned on the radio. When I was finished cleaning in the kitchen I moved into the living room. As I walked into the living room, knocking started on all 4 walls. So I, returned to the kitchen and turned up the volume on the radio. Once I had left the living room, I noticed that the knocking had stopped.

When, I returned it started again. This went on for a good hour then abruptly stopped. After making numerous trips back and forth trying to drown out the knocking by using the radio. After that it was quite until I left at 2 am.

About a week later, I was home alone, when I had another experience. It was around 6 pm, I was changing the liner in the trash can. I looked up and saw this man walk from the living, through the kitchen, in to the back bedroom. He appeared to be in a hurry and had his head turned away from me.

After trying to make heads or tails of what had just happened, I followed him into the bedroom, where he was no where to be found. The patio doors and all the windows were locked from the inside. He just disappeared without a trace... I described the man to my boyfriend and some members of his family.

Unfortunately, they didn't have a clue to who the person could be. I haven' t seen him since.

Green Lady Bridge
Buddha, In.

There are two legends that go with this bridge. Both concern a car wreck. One was that of a girl running late for her prom night curfew. It was a stormy night, a perfect setting. Anyway, she skidded off the side of the bridge and was killed.

The other tale was that of a woman and her daughter crossing the bridge. It too was on a stormy night. They slid off the side of the bridge and both drown.

Now the haunting is as follows:

1. You with some friends drive to the middle of the bridge. Turn off the vehicle. One person gets out and yells, " Green Lady" 3 times. She is suppose to appear.

2. You with some friends drive to the end of the bridge. Everyone in the back-seat gets out. Meanwhile, those in the front seat remain and cross over the bridge and back to the others. Those waiting on the opposite side of the bridge may see a glowing green figure in the back-seat. Those in the car may see her by looking in the rear view mirror.

3. You with some friends drive to the middle of the bridge. Turn off the vehicle and flash your headlights three times. She is to appear in front of the car screaming for help to find her daughter. She'll disappear when she runs over to the side of the bridge.

My friends and I decided on doing number one. All went well until we stopped in the middle of the bridge and it was time for someone to get out. I volunteered. I'm guessing it was about 11 pm. I got out and yelled "Green Lady" 3 times.

As, I went to sit back in the car, I found myself frozen. It felt like someone was standing directly behind me. I asked those in the car to look behind me. Once, I was told that nothing was there, it kind of broke the moment and I was able to sit down. We then left very quickly.

County Line
Martin County, In.

I heard about this house through a source I found to be unreliable. The story that I was told was changed several times. Give or take a few details. The last three families that lived in the house supposing hung themselves with fan belts from railroad spikes in the kitchen ceiling.

By the time my source kept "updating" me on what they were calling the house's history. The suicides had taken place in the kitchen, living room, and then the family room.

I decided to check it out anyway. I have no history of this location. I did however, encounter many cold spots. On film, I found several globes, majority of them on the front porch. In what I'm guessing to be the kitchen / dining room I felt a belt of energy swirling around me.

One visit I'll never forget was when I sensed that belt of energy again this time it seemed to lead me through the kitchen to the back door and disappeared once it crossed the threshold into the woods in the back yard. The house has slid off its foundation and rests against a small hill. With woods so thick, to continue an investigation, you would need a chain saw.

The attic window holds an image that some say is the face of a young boy. Others who have seen it claim that its a misery old man. Anyone can see it, being in plain view. In reality it is really nothing more than a stain in the wood, covering the attic window. Or is it?

Vickie Lee Johnson

About the Author

Vickie Johnson moved to Bedford, Indiana with her parents, brother, and sister in May 1994. Her father had retired from the Navy after twenty years and thought it best to settle close to family. Within that twenty year span Vickie has seen many places and encountered a lot of strange things. Although these events were taking place around her, she didn't really count them as "Paranormal." Until later…since moving to Bedford, she has graduated high school at Bedford North Lawrence. Become a full time Certified Nursing Assistant. Earned diplomas in parapsychology, astrology and psychology through the Stratford Career Institute.

She has found the working in a nursing home has more less gave her interest a boost. You are bound to hear a few ghost stories working in such a field. In time activity began to surface and co-workers began to speak up. Soon Vickie too, was experiencing things that she couldn't explain. Thankfully, she had witnesses to assure her that it wasn't "all in her head." These occurrences inspired her to write this book. She has addressed encounters from early on when her father was transferred throughout the states. Then with a little help, research, and ghosthunting on her part, she has compiled this treat for you. Enjoy!

www.ingramcontent.com/pod-product-compliance
Lightning Source LLC
Chambersburg PA
CBHW030356290526
45785CB00004B/1781